I DO METAPHORS

POEMS

YVONNE ONAKEME ETAGHENE

egberi

I DO METAPHORS

Published by:
EGBERI

Printed in the United States of America

ISBN: 979-8-9908662-8-7 $19

dedicated to every version of myself
I have ever been
and ever will be

poems

guava

for most of my life I had no idea what a guava was
until one manhattan morning a couple years ago I tasted it
knew that gritty, sweet, grainy flavor but not the name
the taste catapulted me back to my childhood in Nigeria
Lagos streets saturated with masquerade costumes scary enough to make
my feet race for cover faster than thudding heart thunder beats
palm leaf skin palm oil blood
red soil sizzling to a slow boil
home
that I've spent so many years away from,
my Ijaw-Urhobo soul feels translated into english/shoved onto highlife turntables
expected to spin/instead just excessively literate in everything
but what's indigenous to my skin.
the afrobeat hip hop on the vinyl of me djs the remix that is my home
where the sound of my own voice grates like a stranger's in my ears
oyibo returning home, abi?

sweet bitter syrup-thick malt
aricocoa-spiced ogbono soup
never feeling Nigerian enough
sugarcane-lined dusty roads
agege bread soft as freshly picked afro
traffic gridlocked on the go slow
it's the go slow cuz you go slow on it
a symphony of shouts and curses is my afrobeat Naija lullaby
home

after 10 black ice-coated syracuse winters,
4 corn field-frozen oberlin winters,
4 brick new york city winters
I   swan   flew   tiptoed   ran
home
relative after relative came by to visit, I disappoint
them
they want computers, ipods, dollars
I want hugs, to dance, eat egusi soup, eba.
I wrap my pain in ankara and cowrie shells
they want to know when I'm getting married, they worry I have no children
I want to hear stories about family that I forgot I knew
like guava
immigration to america has you
forgetting who you are/then remembering
then never feeling good enough
home

like

unbuttered toast

a broken zipper

cold tea

a clasp
with a gap
on a necklace
that won't close

that post it note
with that thing I wrote
that I can't remember
that said everything
I'm tired of feeling

the persistent drip
in the kitchen sink
that no repairwoman
can fix

the rage of a million heartaches
muted & amplified
by the million and first one

hesitant rain on wednesday

pen sprinting races
then breathless
running out of ink

finishing what you
reluctantly began

no one telling you

what’s right
stopped mattering
last sunday

the fortune cookie with useless advice

snow too stubborn to melt in the presence of sun

like
this

another

another set of tears arriving (on track 1, track 1)

I cried so many tears
the sky asked me to borrow some
so she could rain on some faraway city's drought

so many tears
I barter with waterfalls, hot springs and oceans

sling liquid to the thirsty on ferries that float on my **melancholy** to get from sea to not-so-shining sea
I got plenty
more than enough for your garden, your pool and most water sports
lakes, rivers and streams be emailing me
asking for some of my waves & swagger
I mean (they ask) how do you flow like the water
and spit all that fire?
the same way I laugh with sadness
& find joy in my madness
it's tiring sweetie but I don't know how else to be

if I could bottle this shit
we'd run out of bottles

I got enough flow to put tap water out of business
messenger my water to you via poetry
or my poetry via water
water express, confessions that drip drip and drop it like it's ***liquid*** bricks
this is the business of my flow
it's a literal lyrical water flow

and it's kinda salty
like me
my poem is not here to make friends with you
just here to tell you your reflection is in the surface of me
and within the depths
so if you're a friend to yourself
then I guess you're a friend to this flow

I don't have pretty answers
I don't have solutions
I don't have positive thinking or hope
my faith has worn thin
I don't have anything but a lot of salty water
and an absorbent life soaking it up
I don't have joy to sprinkle here
I don't even have another rhyme
I have water and no containers
I have no sugar and a bitter lime
I guess I had one more rhyme in me

at the hospital today

The nurse answered my mother's question without looking at her.
She looked at me instead.
How does that make sense to anyone with a brain or manners or home training?

I wanted to slap her.

I asked her to address my mother.
Since my mother asked the question.
This is not the DMV. These are people's lives you're dealing with.
My mum has an accent. She speaks english just fine. Address her.
Today is the day you learn to respect my immigrant mum.
At least while I'm in the room
At least.

ocean

seashell-sized 4-year-old hand
swallowed within
the ocean of his

on his graduation day,
my dad,
red and black
cap and gown
my small body barely higher than his knees

I don't remember that day
I've seen that photograph
of his ocean swallowing my seashell
so many times it feels like a memory
but I don't remember

I did not wear a cap and gown on *my* graduation day
I rocked traditional Naija clothes my mama gave me
he wasn't there
my mother was
no photographic evidence to capture a moment I forgot
he just wasn't there
he did not know I survived Oberlin
spit passionate poems into bull horns
did not know I embodied verses that took flight

or sparked fire from dimming embers
he wasn’t there on my graduation day
or on thousands of other days
without ceremony to name them.

that old photograph is evidence of a father.
I have no memories of my parents and I
in the same room
not one
the pictures I have in my albums
capture my dad
when I look for what’s missing

when nothing is real
except in a memory
I create thru my mother's eyes
behind the camera

full body crown

body brown. actual color.
not some metaphorical solidarity shade of brown
to be claimed in self-righteous poems, at rallies
or to prove a point
then conveniently set aside in boardrooms,
during job interviews, to the NYPD.
I do not pass for anything but a Black woman
before most see African, they see brown, label me Black
not midnight, not the iris of all our eyes
but the Nina Simone Mississippi Goddamn, Billie Holiday Strange Fruit
black. with a lowercase b.
BROWN. all caps. actual color.
earth and me: same shade tint gradation of hue
my pigment painted by sunrays beamed into me inside mama's belly
my brown: my full body crown
it took years to get here
years of being called burnt toast. too black. too dark. ugly. pretty for a dark skinned girl.
he introduced himself saying: *I don't usually talk to dark skinned girls but…*
you different
compliment with a fist in the middle of it
you know what, I don't usually talk to self-hating pricks—
matter of fact, I still don't. also, I'm a dyke.
nobody ever had to tell you yellow is beautiful
I don't really fuck with light girls but she pretty for a light skinned girl.
I am not your chocolate whatever, brotha
you really think you the first to liken me to cocoa?
my body a rainbow.
peanut butter speckled upper left arm
earth brown belly, bark brown elbows
I want my babies to be brown. sunkissed and brown. eating their own fists. and brown. and to know they're beautiful because I cuddle with them
not cuz somebody reassures them

with trendy t-shirt *brown is beautiful* affirmation

body BROWN.
all caps.
actual
color.

bar

set the bar high
let your guard down

Dyke Winter Scientist

Sometimes I think I'm a born again scientist
I want things to fit into formulas and schedules
To be predictable and quantifiable.
When is it appropriate to fall in love? Make love for the first time?
How many times a week is too much to talk to a new lover?
When do you introduce them to your friends? To how many at a time?
Over dinner?
At a party?

Give me a fuckin formula!
I want all variables to be taken into account.
Her eye color,
how we met,
how I feel on a rainy day in her arms,
the taste of her pussy
Throw these all in the cauldron.
Wait 25 minutes
Then spit out a printout with all the answers.
And while you're at it,
tell me how to feel,
tell me how to heal from lingering trauma from my past,
tell me how to not fuck up a really good thing cuz I'm paranoid she'll hurt me or I won't be enough or this won't be enough

But right now.
It's enough,
it's what I want.
And
I couldn't find a formula online,
couldn't find an equation to calculate the poems she gives me with
her eyes

My breath has no weight,
her touch has no height,
the space our bodies occupy is light,
is felt deeply, is just right,
is steady and I,

I am whole.
Whatever hurt me is *gone*
I'm used to walking with wounds and bruises
so when I look down and there are no scars,
my mind still sees what isn't there.
then I act like I'm headed for heart surgery when I was released from
the hospital
last spring.
I love forward to kickin leaves in the park with you
and winter too
and baby I fuckin hate winter
but I think I could do winter.

With you.

so fly

my smile makes rain dance upward
inspires wallflowers to occupy spotlight
my kiss
cascades constellations of goosebumps
over my lover's skin
that lick through air
whirling hurricanes of thought to our descendants
that womanifest in other dimensions
as glitter and music
the blink of my eyelashes ignite fireflies into flight
angels sing my name
instead of amen
I am so fly
poems spend their lives
sweet talking muses
so they can write
me
oceans backspin and uprock on beaches
to the beat of my hips,
the universe gets lost in my dimensions
and rain drops spark into rivers in my presence

rhymes keep beat to my breath
metronomes ask me to keep time
heartbeats syncopate to my steps

I don't check microphones, mics check me

I proofed rakim's master plan
the mathematical sum
of the numerological value of this poem
erases dozens of "your mama so ugly"
into factors of "our sistas so beautiful"
colors my laughter beams
are vibrant enough to expand the rainbow you kiss in
dictionaries define themselves according to the syntax of my flow
I invent words & eliminate the need for them
languages constantly apologize to me
for not being able to articulate my wonder

my poems began before I existed
I was dancing in my mama's womb
to rhythms
my mama's blood taught me

your name

your heart wide as moon and sun
holding hands rising together
soul delicate as talcum powder slow motion floating in air

oak tree solid
I used to know you
you, all I love in one person
faith unwavering in the face of bills higher than
mountains stacked on top of each other
these days you teeter totter between fragile and frail
doctor's orders: you can't work anymore
the money I send home is never enough
the years, the regret, your pain eat at you
have you lash out at me with verbal whips that slice.
temperamental casting director, you cast me
as horrible daughter who disappoints on Tuesday
savior who is God-sent on Sunday

your palms and fingers used to
knit and knead my favorite foods onto plate
despite arthritis/now
your birthday looms
a hollowed out holiday
everyday, heartache that predates my birth
kickboxes discordant beatboxes

inside your chest
and I want to fix it
you taught this brave warrior bird flight
but when my flight plans take me out of your sky,
it feels like I left you earthbound as I lick clouds

my poems all start and end with you
regardless of whether your name appears on the page
I can't spend time on the phone with you
every phone call with you, my chest caves in, anxious
as you zig zag between hysterical and withdrawn faster than I can
inhale exhale

your arms a well-worn wrappa I sleep and cook in
when you move, your skeleton a rickety sculpture of what the years
did to you
a life full of didn'ts and missing
your name written on the inside of my skin
blistering

cliff

dancing courage enough to fly off cliffs
with no net

I left you and Syracuse behind like footsteps
receipts
mistakes

as

these tears
this heartache

as constant as this heartbeat
as constant as this breath

to a poet i know

i dance like lovemaking
i make love like dancing
i write poems like cooking
i cook poems
i am everything i pray will be sent to me in the form of my wife
so
i me wed, my love, i me wed

first thing

first thing
in the morning,
I need something warm in my mouth
your tongue
or
a cup of tea

all these poems I write about these women
where will they go.
what will I do with them.
will I boil and eat them.
freeze and dry them them.
vacuum pack/seal them
            for later consumption.
put them in a museum
of my own making to later
marvel at.

            I wonder.
maybe I can wear them
dress myself up in them
paint my face with all the apologies
the I didn't mean tos
and the I'm sorry you were hurts
I've collected over the years
here I am
dressed up in poems and apologies…
do I look pretty baby?

late night

before bed
I undress.

first thing
in the morning
I want you
(in my mouth)

untitled

you taught me love is sacrifice and longing
so
I spent my life as if on stage
loving characters who proved you right

skin into verse

sometimes you have to write
even if every syllable hurts
to etch
onto page
sometimes

sometimes you have to write the poem
that rips your ribcage open
exposes off-beat on-beat polyrhythmic heart murmurings
that speak in tongues

sometimes you have to
spill splash crash
hard
against brick walls
so hard the cement sticks to you
and you
tumble
shattered
to ground
and just
lay there

sometimes you feel like death
like every breath
is a surprise
because the ripped open ribcage didn't kill you

sometimes
you cry more tears
than water you drank
that day

sometimes no one will understand
and there will be no witnesses to what you've endured
but your own bedroom walls

and the cells in your body

sometimes you have to kiss your own wounds
and make it better
and I know it's not fuckin fair
or right
but sometimes, that's how the fuck it is

sometimes
you will lose more people than you can count
and sometimes
you will have to let them go
into cemeteries
literal
or otherwise

sometimes
you have to write yourself love poems
turn skin into verse
sometimes
you have to believe in something
greater
than the pain that has taken stubborn residence
inside your bones

sometimes.

there are

there are poems you write
& then there are the ones too stubborn to tame
they roam & wander
lost and found unto themselves

most days
my heads pounds
tears
I don't eat breakfast until dinner time

I am comprised of 19 stubborn poems that defy the pen the typewriter the laptop the freestyle

there are poems you write
and there are poems that write you

sundays

sundays were made for fuckin you

BLOOD

the thug in me like
you can't let a bitch mean this much to you

it's dangerous

but it's too late
there's nothing I can do now
I can't un-love you

I don't have the energy to be optimistic
but I don't know how to live if everything is a tragedy waiting to happen

please don't let me need more than I give
please don't let me dream more than I live

so scared to burden you with my needs I take care of you till I bleed
nurture you with my whole soul
open my bones
let you eat my marrow
is that me loving you
or me letting you kill me
you can't survive like this
you can't keep living like this
letting the whole world build their freedom on your back
swallow and hide your tears so they never see your hurt
until one day you collapse
explode
both
more
and *"no one saw it coming"*
they called the shine in your eyes spirit
not a cry for help
not literally glistening tears about to skydive out of you
they need you strong
so they can lean on you

they're invested in your success so they can eat too
don't mistake a bloodsucker for a blood relation
don't let a taker take you from you,
take your
soul
ambition
time
smile
orgasms
peace of mind

if I don't answer my phone, I don't answer my phone, leave me alone,
give me space

they all surprised I was in the hospital
thoughts of suicide dominating my brain
everyone loves you when you say yes
turn cold when you say no
demand explanations they don't deserve
haven't earned
(for you protecting
your space, energy, peace, magic, SANITY)
my nigga
no is a complete sentence
I owe no one
except myself
my mama
my children
if you mad,
stay mad
I no go die for you
my life bigger than you
bigger than this
I take my lesson
sweet
or bitter pill
grow
pray
cry

pray
move on
pray
glow the fuck up.

Nigerian Dyke Holy Text

I am not: *exotic* *striking* *pretty for a dark skinned girl*
not the cunt that will enable you to fuck your way into a more authentic African existence
I see you not seeing me
hearing I'm Nigerian somehow makes me an original specimen
for your Black nationalist, Pan Africanist consumption
I am not your pussy-flavored passport to finding yourself
my DNA will *not* set you free.
I am Nigerian
not a one-dimensional caricature of who you need an African to be

a hard femme dyke
constellation-colored acrylic nails, baggy jeans,
purple stilettos, sandy timbalands, loose fitting button down, silk neck tie

I eat meat, grilled, bbq'd & stirfried
I am not vegan just because I'm a frohawk-rockin artist
this is not a hairstyle, fad or trend
my hair defies gravity, reaches for Goddess' residence
an expression of my spiritual ascension

I get to the point
tough Nigerian, New York gully
I am passionate: words tougher than fists, softer than peach fuzz
not: *too angry* *hostile* *combative* *with an attitude* *mad for no reason*
I have plenty of reasons
I am not your "teachable moment", not here to educate you like some mobile Nigerian wikipedia app you input dumbass questions into

Of course I speak English
that's what British colonial rule will fuckin do to you
Nigerians pretending to be British, shoving away their indigenous

I’ve been
writing this poem my whole life
everytime someone asked me some bullshit question
I’d recite this
murmuring Nigerian dyke holy text to myself
to remind myself why I exist
I am definition-creating, verbal rocket launcher, melter of glass, lover of her
        who wonders
how long it would take you to see me
        person with insecurities
        a mama, a daddy
        stuffed animals, favorite foods
as human

sundays also

sundays also were made for making love to you, my beloved

<u>**my 5'11" poem without an ending**</u>

you said you wanted to see what I've written about you.
I thought
how can I show you when what I painted doesn't resemble you?
not the way it should
not the way you look at me
the way you mumble good morning
eyes half open, reaching for me
how you slide your fingers inside me like a whisper in the dark
how you massage the part of me that's in pain
the way you hold me,
hard and soft at the same time
how you dice ginger
into perfect tiny little squares

nothing I’ve written
except maybe a line here or there
touches you
as in
begins to do you justice
I wonder
if I’ll read this to you
slow
sitting on the bed
half naked watching your face watch mine as I give you these words
I want to convince you that you’re not poison
that you don’t break things
you make them
I want you to let me into you
all the way

but you’re stubborn

I met you
this 5’11” poem without an ending

paper maché teacup mango soil poem amalgam

I want to write a million little poems
put them in a teacup
drink them

I want to remember you at your best
frame those moments
melt the rest

I want to make paintings larger than me
murals
that feel as intimate as a handwritten letter sent through the mail
from a lover

I want to forget the bad
treasure the good
selective amnesia like that is dangerous
and responsible for why my body stayed when my spirit wanted to go

your fingertips are made of flower petals
and dew drops
your words paper maché images that dance and do cartwheels in my
head

you are as soft as cinderblocks
as sexy as pollination

broken hearted poets are as common as sidewalk cracks
sometimes we are mango pits
drying out on windowsills
the fleshy orangeyellow fruit we once inhabited only a memory
pit not in the earth, sitting there

full of potential wasted

when there’s so much to plant
why do we spend so much time
out of soil?

still

where you wound me
it still bleeds some nights

very very soft

I need something very very soft right now
soft music soft hands soft touches feathers
breeze light tickle me please
eat me till I cry

Hands hands hands hands hands hands
Fingerprints.
Pressure.
Indentations. Of fingertips.
Pressure
of thumbs,
fingertips against skin,
throat,
waist.

Delicate.

Unraveling of clothes.
Garments
falling to floor.

Time Travel
Yvonne Onakeme Etaghene

there is nowhere i will not travel to for you

express train to the moon

pluto

venus

entering a place i never knew
but knew
eating clouds there
sipping slowly on the oceans inside myself

there is nowhere i will not travel to
for you

You
who took it upon yourself to know the mountain blocking your path
Only to find the mountain you thought bigger than you
was, in actuality,
a small-scale version of the topography
inside your index finger.

i found you
after years of searching, i found you

without knowing I was searching, i found you
inside the ink of the tattoo within my skin.

sometimes the stories we tell ourselves
about ourselves
do not do our magic justice

when i called for a love that was in fact beneath me
prayed for a love that was in fact too small for me
this is how it came to be
that i found myself finding myself **found**
crying in front of a mountain i could not pass through
go around
a mountain too high to climb

that was the beginning of the dimension i call, simply,
FOUND.

finding myself found,
i left things i came to understand held me back
Felt.
what who where i left
held the most precious parts of me.

when i
began to travel
into vast galaxies far away from my physical residence, i found
myself
floating
surfing
laughing
free
resting
at ease
        this solace.

of venus.
of galaxies.
without names.
in any language.
any of us know

this place? home
home beyond home

a resting place
a dancing space
rest.
breathing space
rest

Escape from planet earth.
Another dimension is where I feel safest.
Alchemize heartache into time travel
Until home is a vibration fast as hummingbird wings.
You can't
see the motion of the wings flapping
but
you know i am flying.

the mountain outside of me became the mountain inside me when I knew any obstacle in front of me must first be faced inside of me

facing the mountains within
melted the mountains before me
opening a glowing portal shimmering like a tourmaline crystal in the sunlight
an invitation
to come home to another home

the mountain i feared
is a home.
Imagine.
The thing you fear becoming your best friend.

there is nowhere i will not travel to
for you
for me
into me
home

my brown eyes

i want to write something sweet for you
that you may never know is about you/
something solid like a heartbeat
sensual like a swollen clit
but classy
even when i'm raunchy/
i want to give you my words,
a little bit, maybe a hundred or so,
gift you with dark luscious candle lit slow smiling
poetry so delicious
you thought we were just talking
girl, i wanna show you me
not braggadocio
not wit
not intellect or politic
but my soft terrain, my early morning
my sunday sweats
my hour-long baths
my cooking in my mama's wrappa
my brown eyes
& the shyness you might find there
if you look
long enough
to see...
i can be awkward
and intense
funny and innocent.
i don't know
sometimes it ain't got to be marriage-and-kids deep, renting a u-haul
for the first date, emotional codependency,
therapy,
exes
sometimes—
sometimes it's just as simple as
i like you.

kisses in tupperware

your body is a familiar path I've walked a thousand times to my favorite place.

it's february
and I am kissing you for may today,
kissing you for next tuesday,
for next month, for a few hours from now when you are sleeping in mount vernon,
miles away from me in harlem. I put your kisses in tupperware to be devoured later in a hungry moment. you asked me why I was kissing you like I was never going to see you again; you told me for a long time, I am all you have known and wanted. I started crying.

I think people see you as calm and reserved but I know you love, know your love as full of fire and heat. I know your passion, *I know you,* when your tongue is diving into me, your hands tight around my waist, your body arching into mine, your moans loud, your lips a dark pink, your teeth biting into me, I know you there, like that, full of heat, spilling onto my body, your fingers fast, your words pouring into my ear painting wet, lustful choreography our bodies dance out on this bed. *I know you like that.*

what is this they say about letting go? *let go?*
I am the hold on queen, the clutter princess, the gonna-keep-this-just-in-case-I-need-it-someday lady. I keep things closer than people; I have walked away from many women but you I want to keep ever so close to me.
neither one of us wants to let go of us,
we hold on when it hurts, take breaths, step back, come back, make love, cook, touch, laugh, scream.
you and I–
how many poems have been born between us?
in agony, desire, bliss? our lips
have uttered many pretty, ugly things–some of the pretty
and many of the ugly things were mine, I admit.
my love,
you are my family,

I have cried before you tears no one else has seen and tonight
my fingers sketch these words searching for meaning, *I will not let you go*, I pray for the strength to trust that I do not have to hold onto us so tightly, I pray for the clarity to trust we will still be *love*,
my love
even if we are not lovers.

volcano

Brooklyn. August 2005. Rooftop.

I asked my former lover:
do you still love her?

she said:
I don't know.

I
stopped
everything.

don't touch me!!! don't fuckin touch me you confused bitch!!!

a former friend of mine said to me:
"fly, not everyone is strong enough to love a volcano…there are parts of me that are in love with you and parts of me that are not brave enough to love you"
I wanted to scream:
FUCK YOU!!!
{but I wrote this instead}

I wonder who volcanoes make love to,
who makes love to the ones in Hawai'i?
who comforts her,
who tells her she is beautiful?
when she feels an eruption coming
does rain rain
attempting to muffle her fire?
does she get tired of everyone expecting fire
when she feels icy?
this volcano feels icy
& if you came for the heat today there are ice cubes falling out of my palms
& dripping down my spine

because I've had enough of
you thinking you know who I am and what I'm about,
you decided I was fierce and you weren't
so you could live down to your lowest misinterpretation of your fuckin destiny/
admiring me
is a carefully chosen distraction
from all you are scared to be
I sometimes volcano, sometimes monsoon or hurricane, tornado, torrential rains, earthquake,
also: still lake…calm breeze…falling leaf
you act like I'm your mama
or your grandmamma
with a switch ready to tear your ass up the way you so scared of committing to me/
I'm glad I was the one
to break you in for the next one you'll finally get your *tired ass* together for
you love what I do and who I am because I'm so—
brave/beautiful/talented/bold/amazing/intelligent/daring
blah blah fuckin blah.
I don't care
there are nights I would forfeit your admiration
for arms that held me
from dusk past dawn
honestly
when God was passing out the colorful adjectives that we'd have to live our lives by
I must've been bleeding my kids away in the bathroom
because if I had known my "volcano" would cause me such chosen and unchosen solitude
maybe I would have opted for adjectives like
weak
quiet
submissive
fucked up
directionless
indecisive
selfish

self-centered
something conspicuously flawed enough to garner me/a long lasting relationship
maybe it's not that I'm *too* explosive
too sensitive
too much
too intense
maybe it's just that you're not fierce enough *for me.*

like dawn, like dew

{love poem to my friends}

i love you like the breath i was born with, you are the song i move with.
this poem in my bones is for you
you make me feel like sky, like honey, like red soil in my homeland feels on my feet
i love you like dawn loves to yawn good morning
like dew loves the blades of grass she always returns to
the moment you enter my arms, i feel at home, i feel like who i always was but needed you to remind me, you give me hallelujah and amen all day
you bring me bliss without even trying and i love you
with a tremendous tenderness these words don't do justice.

passion fruit
(to the daughter i may never meet)

remember me baby? *my baby.* it's been a long time since we spoke, so much has happened. so much healing and heartache, growth, confusion and clarity. yeah i'm not with your other mama anymore, still love her, maybe she was never your other mama, maybe i was meant to be mama enough to be your 2 mothers? wonder what your eyes would look like, if you'd be tall like me, a smart mouth like me, wonder if you'd be as stubborn as me. sometimes you seem like a poem in the flesh, well, the spirit.

i'm pretty clear that i'm never gonna have you, *beautiful you.* offer my breast to you to feed you, teach you about love, show you how to write a poem, fry plantain, crochet, dance. you puzzle me, this puzzles me, motherhood puzzles me. i don't want to hurt you, i don't want to mess up, don't think i have the patience to love you proper. my insecurities are talking.

in the absence of you in my arms, let me tell you what i'd teach you if you were here.

i will write you poems in the absence of you.

love,
mama

dream

I am who I dreamt I could be
before I knew I could be
that dream

Thank You

I thank you so deeply for your time and attention.
I appreciate you so much.
Thank you and thank you again.

Much Love,
~Y.

Acknowledgments

"Time Travel" was previously published in Aster(ix)'s Winter 2021-2022 in-residency series, The Amaranta Project.

"your name" was previously published in Walking the Tightrope: Poetry and Prose by LGBTQ Writers from Africa (Anthology, Lethe Press, 2015).

Biography

Yvonne Onakeme Etaghene is an Ijaw and Urhobo Nigerian dyke poet, performer, author, dancer, playwright, visual artist, and fashion designer.

Her writing has been published in journals, anthologies and poetry chapbooks including: *afrocrown: fierce poetry* (2000), *write or die* (2004), *tongue twisted transcontinental sista* (2006), *skin into verse* (2014) and *skin into verse: a remix* (2021).

In 2012, Etaghene founded Sugarcane, an LGBTQ+ BIPOC writing workshop series that centers LGBTQ+ African, Latin/o, Indigenous, Asian, immigrant and immigrant- descendant literary and performative voices. The eight-week curriculum culminates in a community performance showcase.

Etaghene has presented her visual art in solo and group visual art exhibitions and established a fashion line called *OyinT. Designs by Yv. Etaghene*, which explores the relationship between Nigerian aesthetics, gender expression, and self-acceptance. Additionally, Yvonne hosts the NIGERIAN DYKE REALNESS Podcast, a space where she discusses mental health, art, and politics as it relates to and impacts African queer women and gender nonconforming people.

From 2021 to 2023, Etaghene was a Svane Family Foundation Inaugural Artist in Headlands Center for the Arts' Bay Area Fellowship Program. In 2023, she was honored as a WESTAF BIPOC Artist Fund Awardee. Etaghene received a Bachelor of Arts degree from Oberlin College, a Master's degree from New York University, and a Master of Fine Arts in Creative Writing from Antioch University, Los Angeles.

EMERGENCY CONTACT, a film directed, written by and starring Yvonne Onakeme Etaghene, premieres June 2024.

EVERYTHING: www.myloveisaverb.com
FASHION: www.oyintdesigns.com
PODCAST: www.nigeriandykerealness.com

www.ingramcontent.com/pod-product-compliance
Lightning Source LLC
LaVergne TN
LVHW011050110826
845149LV00015B/3445

* 9 7 9 8 9 9 0 8 6 6 2 8 7 *